In 1715 French soldiers constructed Fort St. Philippe de Michilimackinac. This fortified community, commonly called Michilimackinac, became the great fur trade center of the Northwest until its abandonment in 1781. It was here where fur traders and Indians rendezvoused, French and British officers organized war parties, and explorers began their journeys into the vast western unknown.

The Site and its Inhabitants

In 1960, the Mackinac Island State Park Commission began reconstructing Fort Michilimackinac. With plans based upon historical and archaeological research, workmen rebuilt the soldier's barracks and erected part of the stockade which encloses the fort.

To finance this program, the Commission sold revenue bonds. Since then, admission fees have been used to repay the bonds, to reconstruct more buildings, to continue archaeological and historical research, and to interpret and to maintain the site. Michilimackinac is being reconstructed to look as it did in the mid-1770's.

Soldiers Barracks

Originally built in 1769 by a contractor from New York; moved to Mackinac Island in 1781; Reconstructed in 1960.

The barracks with its large brick chimnies was one of the forts more substantial buildings. Erected on a stone foundation, the horizontal logs are pegged into upright posts. A hipped shingle roof covers the barracks which housed seventy-two soldiers.

Michilimackinac's main interpretive museum is located inside.

The Rue Dauphine (Street of the Princess) runs the length of the fort from land gate to water gate.

Silver Tenth Regiment of Foot officer's button found at Michilimackinac.

3

Southwest Rowhouse

Originally built mid-eighteenth century; Reconstructed in 1968.

Three families lived in this bark roofed row house. Built in the steep roof French fashion, the house has walls of upright logs, chinked with mud while the end is wattle and daub.

The house was originally longer, but the end houses were dismantled to make a garden.

At the rear of the house are individual yards divided by cedar picket fences. The house backs on the Rue Diable (Street of the Devil).

Augustin Langlade owned the middle house during the 1740's. Later French and British traders and officers resided here.

Laurent Du Charme

Born: 1723,
Montreal, Canada
Died: after 1787

Laurent Du Charme began a modest fur trading career at Michilimackinac in 1754. Four years later his wife Marguerite Amable Metivier and daughter moved from Montreal and lived with him in his house on the Rue Diable. There in 1760, twin sons Louis and Pierre Augustine were born.

Du Charme traded at Milwaukee and Green Bay in the late 1760's and the 1770's. In 1777 serving as Captain Arent De Peyster's agent at Milwaukee Du Charme kept an eye on the Potawatomi Chief Siggenauk "Black Bird" who had allied himself with the Spanish.

Due to a shortage of trade goods in 1779, Du Charme joined other Michilimackinac merchants in a General Store. They pooled their resources and shared the profits. By this time Du Charme's family had returned to Montreal although he continued to trade at Michilimackinac.

Alexis Sejourné *dit* Sans Chagrin

Alexis Sejourné dit Sans Chagrin served as sergeant of the French troops at Michilimackinac from at least 1749 to 1760. His wife Marie Angelique Tareau, gave birth to a daughter, Angelique, baptized in Ste. Anne's Church on 11 March, 1749. Sixteen years later, Sans Chagrin and Marie Angelique were godparents when Angelique's baby was baptized.

During the attack of 1763, a tomahawked British soldier crashed through the door of Sans Chagrin's house. British trader Henry Bostwick later accused him of standing by idly while Indians and Frenchmen plundered the Englishman's property.

Like many other soldiers, Sans Chagrin also engaged in the Indian trade. After the British assumed control of Michilimackinac, he became a full time trader. During the 1770's, he wintered among Ottawa and Potawatomi living along the Grand River (Michigan).

Charlotte-Ambrosine Bourassa

Born: 1735,
La Prairie, Canada
Died: 1818 (?),
Green Bay, Wisconsin

Charlotte-Ambrosine Bourassa, daughter of fur trader René Bourassa, grew up in the family house on the corner of Rue de Babillarde and Rue Dauphine.

On 12 August, 1754, she married Charles Langlade in Ste. Anne's Church. Father Marie Louis Le Franc performed the ceremony before the community's leading citizens.

She and Charles had two daughters; Charlotte Catherine, born in 1756 at their winter camp at the Grand River, and Louise Domitille born three years later at Michilimackinac.

During her adult life at Michilimackinac, Charlotte served as a witness to numerous baptisms and was godmother to several infants.

Fearful of Indians, she reluctantly left Michilimackinac in 1763 when her family moved to Green Bay. There she lived the rest of her life.

Charles Langlade

Born: 1729, Michilimackinac
Died: 1800 or 1801,
Green Bay, Wisconsin

Charles Langlade was the son of Augustin Langlade, a prominent trader, and Domitilde, the sister of Ottawa Chief La Fourche. On 12 August 1754, in Ste. Anne's Church at Michilimackinac, he married Charlotte Bourassa.

When only 10 years old, he accompanied La Fourche on the Chickasaw campaign. The Ottawa credited their victory to a special spirit which protected young Charles. Thereafter, the Indians held him in awe.

During the 1763 attack, Langlade courageously rescued Captain George Etherington and Lieutenant William Leslie from hostile warriors. Later that year he moved his family to Green Bay.

Throughout the American Revolution, Langlade recruited and led Indian war parties in support of the British war effort.

When he was not leading war parties, Langlade engaged in the fur trade. He established a winter post along the Grand River at Grand Haven, Michigan in 1755 and traded there until 1790.

Church of Ste. Anne de Michilimackinac

Built in 1743 by Joseph Ainsse; moved to Mackinac Island in 1780; Reconstructed in 1964.

This sturdy log church is constructed of squared horizontal logs which are lapped at the corners. Surmounting the shingle roof is a small steeple which houses a brass bell. A portion of the original bell was found on the site by archaeologists.

The church was the center of religious activities at Michilimackinac.

Today, when the church bell rings, an eighteenth-century wedding is re-enacted.

Ste. Anne's medal found at Michilimackinac

Priest's House – Blacksmith Shop

Originally built in 1740's, Priest's House moved to Mackinac Island in 1780; Reconstructed in 1970.

Joined to the church by a covered passageway, the Priest's house is built of squared timbers dovetailed together at the corners. This reconstruction was based on an existing building on Mackinac Island.

The priest lived here while at Michilimackinac. The blacksmith shop was located close by so that the priest could closely supervise the blacksmith who worked for him.

Blacksmiths were very important people at Michilimackinac because only they could repair and make iron and steel objects. Many gun parts and scraps of metal were found by archaeologists on the site of this shop.

Jean-Baptiste-Ambroise Amiot

Born: 1694, Quebec, Canada   *Died:* after 1763

Jean-Baptiste-Ambroise Amiot served as blacksmith at Michilimackinac for over forty years. He repaired muskets and tools and made ironwork used in the community.

About 1720 he married Marie Anne, a Sac Indian. They had eight children and lived in a house in the northeast corner of the fort across from Joseph Ainsse.

Amiot worked for the Jesuit priest, who possessed a King's Memorial granting him the monopoly of blacksmithing at the post. This created hardship for Amiot and by 1742 reduced him to begging from the local Ottawa. At their request, the Governor-General of New France freed Amiot from his bond to the priest.

Amiot occasionally wintered among the Indians. His son Louis was born at an Indian camp near Chicago in 1745. Twelve years later, Louis died from smallpox during the epidemic at Michilimackinac.

Skilled blacksmiths demonstrate their craft to fascinated visitors.

Pierre Du Jaunay

Born: 1704, Vannes, Brittany, France
Died: 1780, Quebec, Canada

Father Du Jaunay, a devout Jesuit, came to Michilimackinac in 1735. He performed 25 weddings and 120 baptisms in Ste. Anne's Church.

Known for his integrity, it was said he "never told a lie in his life." Consequently, he had great influence among the Ottawa and in the French community.

When the British took control of Michilimackinac, Du Jaunay urged his parishoners to accept the change peacefully. During the Chippewa attack in 1763, he gave refuge to soldiers and traders in his house. Upon the return of British troops in September, 1764, Du Jaunay again pledged his loyalty and worked to re-establish order in the settlement.

The following year, at the direction of his superiors, he closed his Ottawa mission and left Michilimackinac for Quebec.

John Askin

Born: 1739,
Auchanacloy,
Northern Ireland
Died:1818,
Windsor, Canada

John Askin, of Scottish descent, moved in 1758 from Ireland to New York where he engaged in trade at Albany.

Shortly after the British displaced the French, Askin came to Michilimackinac. His principal business was providing provisions and merchandise for fur traders. He owned a fleet of sailing vessels — Welcome, Archange, Mackinac and De Peyster which crisscrossed Lakes Erie, Huron, Michigan, and Superior transporting trade goods and procuring Indian corn from Detroit to Milwaukee. Askin also served as the post commissary and barrack master.

Like many fur traders, Askin had a liasion with an Ottawa woman who bore him three children. In 1773, he married Marie Archange Barthe at Detroit. With this marriage, he forged an alliance with her father, Charles Andrew Barthe, a prominent Detroit merchant. For years Askin and his brother-in-law, John Baptiste Barthe, also operated a post at Sault Ste. Marie.

Corner cupboard in the Piquet House.

Marie Archange Barthe

Born: 1749, Detroit
Died: 1820, Sandwich,
Ontario, Canada

Marie Archange Barthe was the daughter of Charles Andrew Barthe. In 1773, at Detroit, she married John Askin before Commandant Major Henry Bassett and the leading citizens.

Archange moved to Michilimackinac where Teresa, the first of her nine children, was born the following winter. In addition to her own babies, she raised Askin's three other children.

Archange was one of the wealthiest women at Michilimackinac. The social highlight of her stay at Michilimackinac was planning and staging her step-daughter Catherine's wedding to Samuel Robertson in 1778.

When Askin's business failed during the American Revolution, his family moved to Detroit. On 24 July, 1780 Archange, followed by Teresa and little Archange, carried her infant son John Charles on board the Welcome for her return home.

Northwest Rowhouse

Originally built in the 1730's; Askin house was reconstructed in 1962; Piquet and Chevalier houses in 1977.

Houses at Michilimackinac were generally small though sleeping rooms were located upstairs. Overlapping boards were used to roof the Piquet and Chevalier houses.

A wealthy merchant, perhaps John Askin, lived on the site of the Askin house.

Today the Chevalier house serves as the entrance to a unique archaeological tunnel which leads past an original French well and a storage cellar.

Chinese export porcelain and a fine English teapot once graced a Michilimackinac table.

Guardhouse

Originally built in 1751; moved to Mackinac Island in 1781; Reconstructed in 1978.

Built in the style of a typical French guardhouse the building has a broad porch to shelter the sentinel.

Inside, beneath the floor, is the "Black Hole" dungeon where prisoners could be secured.

The Guardhouse was the headquarters for the soldiers on guard duty. Here they ate and slept when not out walking a beat or standing watch at the fort's gates.

English creamware plate dating from the 1770's.

Ezekiel Solomon

Born: Berlin, Germany
Died: 1809, Mackinac Island

Ezekiel Solomon was the first Jew to come to Michigan. He arrived at Michilimackinac in September, 1761, only a short time after Alexander Henry. For the next four decades, Solomon was one of the most prominent traders at the Straits.

During the attack of 1763, the Chippewa took him prisoner. The Ottawa, however, rescued him and finally freed him at Montreal.

In 1769, he married Elizabeth Du Bois, a French Canadian, at Montreal and brought her to Michilimackinac. They had four sons and two daughters. Solomon divided his time between Montreal and Michilimackinac though he spent some winters trading among Indians.

Though a Jew, he pledged in 1778 50 livres towards the support of a Catholic missionary in Michilimackinac. When the fur trade floundered in 1779, Solomon helped found the General Store. During the next year, he moved with the rest of the traders to the new community on Mackinac Island.

Constante Chevalier

Constante Chevalier was the wife of master carpenter Joseph Ainsse and the mother of Joseph Louis Ainsse. Her daughter Marie Coussante, who died on 10 August 1743, was the first person buried beneath Ste. Anne's Church.

A few years later Joseph Ainsse died. Before remarrying, Constante bore two illegitimate children. On 6 July 1751 Father Du Jaunay married her to Francois Louis Cardin, a soldier, who became the post notary.

In 1767, Major Robert Rogers employed her to spy on, and to assist in negotiations with the Ottawa at L'Arbre Croche and the Chippewa at Cheboygan.

La Fourche

Born: c.1715
Died: after 1797

La Fourche was the most prominent chief among the Ottawa at L'Arbre Croche. His sister Domitilde was Charles Langlade's mother.

Closely allied with the French at Michilimackinac, he led a war party against the Chickasaw in 1739 and fought the English throughout the 1740's and 1750's. In 1757, he helped capture Fort William Henry, but the taste of victory turned bitter as many at L'Arbre Croche died from smallpox.

Following the departure of the French authority, La Fourche embraced the English. When the Chippewa captured the fort in 1763, he and his warriors rescued many survivors and escorted them to Montreal.

During the American Revolution, he led British war parties and in August, 1782 helped rout Daniel Boone and an American force at Blue Licks, Kentucky.

Matchekewis

Born: c.1735 Died: c.1805

Matchekewis was chief of a Chippewa band which lived at Cheboygan in summer and near Thunder Bay or Saginaw Bay in winter. A tall man, he weighed over 200 pounds.

He, along with the aged Chief Minavavana, planned and led the attack on Michilimackinac on 2 June 1763. Within a few years, however, Matchekewis became friends with the English.

In 1777, he fought along with General Burgoyne against the Americans at Saratoga.

Matchekewis helped Patrick Sinclair plan and organize the ill-fated attack on the Spanish at St. Louis. As a reward, Sinclair gave him a log house which was moved over the ice from Michilimackinac to the Chippewa village at Cheboygan.

In 1794, Matchekewis fought against the Americans at the Battle of Fallen Timbers in Ohio. Following the American victory, he made peace. As a token of goodwill, he gave Bois Blanc Island in the Straits of Mackinac to the Americans.

Joseph Louis Ainsse

Born: 1744,
Michilimackinac
Died: 1802

Joseph Louis Ainsse was the son of Joseph Ainsse, builder of Ste. Anne's Church, and Constante Chevalier. They lived in a house opposite the northeast bastion, across the street from Jean Baptiste Amiot.

While traveling and living in Indian country, Ainsse learned nine languages. He knew hundreds of Indians personally and was greatly respected by the Ottawa, Chippewa, Potawatomi, Menominee, Winnebago, Sac, and Fox. Most of the time between 1768 and 1790 he was the official Indian interpreter. British officers depended upon him to accurately translate delicate negotiations between themselves and native chiefs.

In 1775, Father Pierre Gibault married Ainsse to Theresa Bondy in the church his father had constructed thirty-two years earlier.

King's Storehouse

Originally built in 1773; moved to Mackinac Island in 1781; Reconstructed in 1961.

The storehouse was built by the soldiers of the Tenth Regiment of Foot upon a firm stone foundation. An earlier structure, whose original stone floored basement can be seen inside, once stood on this site.

Within the storehouse, the commandant stored the soldier's provisions and other merchandise which was given to the Indians as presents.

Brass trade kettles were very popular with the Indians.

Gilded King's Eighth Regiment of Foot officer's buttons.

Commanding Officer's House

Originally built in the 1770's; Reconstructed in 1963.

Erected by the British on the site of an earlier officer's quarters, the house contains two massive stone fireplaces.

Robert Rogers, Arent Schuyler De Peyster and Patrick Sinclair all lived here.

Arent Schuyler De Peyster

Born: 1736, New York, New York
Died: 1822, Dumfries, Scotland

Colonel Arent Schuyler De Peyster arrived at Michilimackinac on 10 July, 1774 with two companies of the King's Eighth Regiment on board the schooner Dunmore. He was from an aristocratic Dutch family in New York and had served in the French and Indian War and in Germany.

Throughout his command, De Peyster worked tirelessly to keep peace among the western Indians and to enlist their loyalty to Britain during the American Revolution. Frequently, he held Indian councils to exchange presents and words. The largest was at L'Arbre Croche on 4 July, 1779.

A friend of the fur trade, De Peyster promoted its prosperity. As a token of their affection for him, Michilimackinac traders presented him with a silver bowl when he left in October, 1779 to assume command at Detroit.

A poet, De Peyster recorded some of his experiences at Michilimackinac in verse. He published these in Miscellanies by an Officer in 1813.

Rebecca De Peyster

Rebecca De Peyster, daughter of Provost Blair of Dumfries, Scotland, accomanied her husband, Arent, to Michilimackinac in 1774. They lived in the Commanding Officer's House. Their love for each other was so deep that they were seldom apart.

Childless, Rebecca lavished much attention on her pets including her favorite "Tim," a chipmunk.

A cultured woman, Rebecca had studied dancing in Edinburgh. As the commandant's wife she was the first lady of the community. Consequently she hosted social gatherings for the town's leading citizens and their wives. Rebecca and her friend Archange Askin and other upper class women regularly gathered to sip tea and to show off their new fashions imported from London.

Arent Schuyler De Peyster

17

Powder Magazine

Originally built in the 1740's; Reconstructed in 1981.

To lessen damage in case it exploded the powder magazine was placed underground. A layer of dirt provided protection from an enemy's flaming arrows.

Originally privately owned, it was taken over by the British garrison. All the fort's gunpowder was stored here.

Archaeologists found the burnt ruins that had been left behind when the British moved the garrison to Fort Mackinac in 1781.

MICHILIMACKINAC BIOGRAPHY

Jupiter Wendell

Jupiter Wendell was a black slave owned by John Askin. Sometime before 1775 Askin purchased him at Albany, New York and brought him to Michilimackinac.

A master cooper, Jupiter fashioned hundreds of barrels needed to ship provisions for voyageurs and to preserve fish salted down for winter consumption. He also made wooden buckets, butter firkins, and wash tubs for the inhabitants of Michilimackinac.

A competent sailor, Jupiter frequently served on the crew of Askin's small sloops Mackinac and De Peyster. Carrying goods from Michilimackinac to Sault Ste. Marie, these vessels were sometimes pulled up the St. Mary's rapids into Lake Superior for a voyage to Grand Portage on the lake's northwestern corner.

Chevalier House

Originally built in the 1730's; Rebuilt in the 1760's; Reconstructed in 1985.

Occupied by French traders, 1730's-1761, British soldiers lived here from 1761 until they tore the house down in 1775.

The British demolished this dilapidated structure because they feared that if it caught fire, the powder magazine next door would be in danger.

The stairways inside the Chevalier House lead to the exhibit of the powder magazine ruins.

Solomon-Levy and British Officer's Houses

Originally built in the 1730's; Rebuilt in the 1760's; Reconstructed in 1989.

The British Officer's House was occupied by French-Canadian fur traders until they rented it to British soldiers in 1761. By the late 1770's, a British officer resided here to protect the entrance to the powder magazine during the American Revolution. It is believed that Lieutenant George Clowes of the King's Eighth Regiment lived here.

The Solomon-Levy House was owned by Pierre Parant for many years before he sold it to Ezekiel Solomon and Gershon Levy in 1765. Solomon and Levy operated their trading post out of the west room and used the east room for living quarters.

19

Alexander Henry

Born: 1739, New Brunswick, New Jersey
Died: 1824, Montreal, Canada

In September 1761 Alexander Henry, disguised as a Frenchman, was the first English trader to reach Michilimackinac. The next spring he visited Sault Ste. Marie and acquired a lasting interest in the area. In 1765 he began trading north of Lake Superior.

During the attack in 1763, Henry hid, but the Chippewa captured him. Wawatam, a minor Chippewa chief, who had adopted him as a brother a year earlier saved Henry's life.

Henry's influence on the Mackinac trade extended far beyond his own career. In the 1780's he introduced John Jacob Astor to the Canadian fur trade, and Astor carried this business to new heights in the nineteenth century.

In 1809 Henry wrote Travels and Adventures in Canada and the Indian Territories Between the Year 1760 and 1776. *It became a classic on Indian life and fur trade. Part one has been reprinted as* Attack at Michilimackinac.

Alexander Henry

René Bourassa

Born: 1688, La Prairie, Canada
Died: 1778, Montreal, Canada

René Bourassa embarked in the western fur trade in 1726. By 1738 his trade centered at Michilimackinac. He supplied wine and provisions for the Chickasaw expedition in 1739 and for Indian negotiations in subsequent years.

His wife Marie Catherine Leriger de la Plante joined him at Michilimackinac in the 1740's. They lived in a house, which faced the parade ground, located on the corner of Rue de Babillarde and Rue Dauphine. Bourassa was an important citizen and served as a witness for many baptisms and weddings.

His sons René and Ignace carried on his trade after 1750. Daughter Charlotte-Ambrosine married Charles Langlade in Ste. Anne's Church on 12 August, 1754.

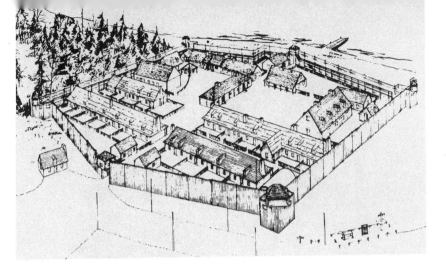

Fort Michilimackinac, 1775

Artist's reconstruction of Michilimackinac in 1775;
Drawn by Victor Hogg.

The eighteen foot high stockade was built from
cedar pickets set in a trench. The enclosure measured
360 feet north-south and 333 feet east-west. On each
corner a bastion with a sentry box jutted out. Additional sentry boxes protected the land and water
gates.

The Land Gate

Here on 2 June, 1763 the Chippewa and Sac Indians
played *baggatiway*. They tossed the ball over the wall,
signaling a sudden attack on the British garrison.

The Water Gate

During summer hundreds of rowdy voyageurs carried thousands of fur packs and bales of trade goods through the water gate. Their large birchbark canoes were drawn up on the beach.

Dutch gin bottle.

Patrick Sinclair

Born: 1736, Lybster, Caithness, Scotland
Died: 1820, Lybster

An officer in the British Army, Patrick Sinclair became attached to the new British fleet on the Upper Great Lakes. In 1764 he was the first captain to sail on Lake Huron since the ill-fated Griffin.

In 1775 Sinclair was appointed Lieutenant Governor for Michilimackinac, but the fortunes of war prevented him from reaching the Straits until 4 October, 1779.

He devoted all his time and energy to moving the community to Mackinac Island and to carrying on the British war effort. Most notably, he organized the party led by Emmanuel Hesse that attacked St. Louis in 1780.

Sinclair spent a fortune outfitting Indians for war and providing food and clothing for their families. He also doled out piles of presents to keep them loyal to the Crown. Overspending his budget, Sinclair was forced to relinquish his command when his superiors refused to honor his expense vouchers.

Throughout his stay, Sinclair embroiled himself in controversy. In July, 1780 he accused Lieutenant Alexander Harrow, commander of the Welcome, of usurping authority and had him arrested. Captain John Mompesson of the King's Eighth came in August, 1780, claiming to be the senior officer. Rejecting this, Sinclair refused to speak to Mompesson. Earlier Sinclair had confiscated John Askin's boats and effectively prevented him from carrying on his business.

Patrick
Sinclair

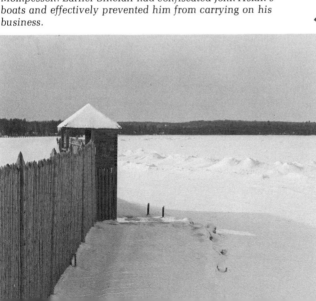

Each winter the Straits freeze over. For several months Michilimackinac was isolated from the rest of the world.

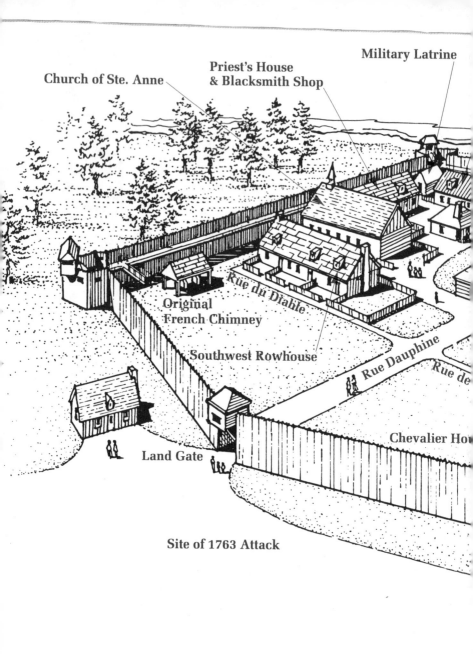

Church of Ste. Anne

Priest's House
& Blacksmith Shop

Military Latrine

Rue du Diable

Original
French Chimney

Southwest Rowhouse

Rue Dauphine

Rue de

Chevalier Hou

Land Gate

Site of 1763 Attack

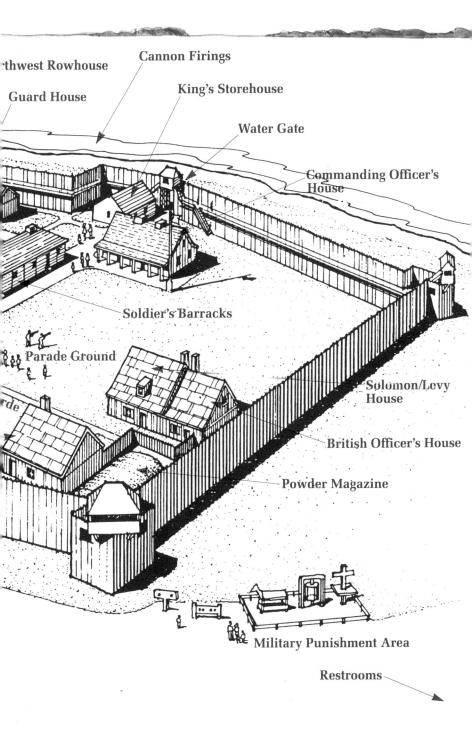

thwest Rowhouse

Cannon Firings

Guard House

King's Storehouse

Water Gate

Commanding Officer's House

Soldier's Barracks

Parade Ground

Solomon/Levy House

British Officer's House

Powder Magazine

Military Punishment Area

Restrooms

The Welcome

John Askin constructed the Sloop *Welcome* at Michilimackinac in 1775. She was fifty-five feet long, had a sixteen foot beam, and was rated at forty-five tons. Armed with two swivel guns and two blunderbusses, she had a crew of eight.

The *Welcome* carried cargo from Fort Erie, located on the eastern end of Lake Erie, to Detroit and Michilimackinac. On board, Askin transported corn and merchandise for fur traders as well as government stores and provisions to maintain the garrison. Among its many passengers were Matchekewis and the black fur trader Jean Baptiste Point du Sable, who had established the first post at Chicago

During the American Revolution the Crown purchased the *Welcome* for £ 900. In summer 1779 the *Welcome*, loaded with provisions, sailed down Lake Michigan following a detachment of troops sent to St. Joseph, but never delivered her cargo. She made numerous trips between Michilimackinac and Mackinac Island moving inhabitant's possessions in 1780 and 1781. Her logbook from 1779-1781 presents a vivid insight into early navigation on the Great Lakes.

Some time in 1781 the *Welcome* was lost with her stores.

Reconstruction of the *Welcome*

Based on extensive research in the United States, England and Canada the *Welcome* has been authentically reconstructed. Construction began in 1973.

Designed by Frederick Ford Jr. and supervised by Ted McCutcheon the vessel came to life under the watchful eyes of more than a million visitors. Skilled boatbuilders labored nearly 40,000 hours to painstakingly recreate this living memorial to the maritime history of the Great Lakes.

The *Welcome* is now being managed by the Maritime Heritage Alliance in Traverse City.

Dark green wine bottle.

The History of Michilimackinac

On the North Side of the Straits

Jean Nicolet, the first Frenchman to see Mackinac Island, paddled his birch bark canoe through the Straits of Mackinac in 1634 enroute to Green Bay. From then on, the French recognized the significance of Mackinac where Lake Huron and Lake Michigan join only a short distance from the entrance to Lake Superior to the northeast. These lakes provided access to the vast western wilderness, home of numerous Indian tribes and fur bearing animals. Furs, to make into beaver hats and luxurious coats, were in great demand in Europe.

In the 1660's, a number of illegal traders called *coureurs de bois* established a fur trading settlement at St. Ignace. There a band of Ottawa had a fortified village, and a band of Huron, fleeing the Iroquois, were soon to join them. On nearby Mackinac Island, Jesuit missionaries Claude Dablon and Jacques Marquette began their ministry to the Huron during the harsh winter of 1670-71. A few months later, Marquette moved the mission to St. Ignace where a mission to the Ottawa was also founded.

Lured by tales of a vast river to the west, Louis Jolliet, Father Marquette, and five men set out from St. Ignace in two canoes on 17 May 1673 in search of the legendary Mississippi River. Their discoveries broadened knowledge of North American geography and spread French influence among Indians living in the upper Mississippi Valley.

On 27 August 1679, René-Robert Cavelier, Sieur de la Salle, aboard the *Griffin* sailed into East Moran bay. Previously, everyone came to St. Ignace by canoe. The *Griffin* proceeded on to an island in Green Bay, picked up a load of furs, and disappeared mysteriously on her return. Over eighty years passed before another sailing vessel plied the Straits.

The English also coveted Michilimackinac's fur trade riches. In 1685, Johannes Roseboom came from Albany, New York by way of Lake Huron, bringing English trade goods to exchange for Huron and Ottawa furs at St. Ignace. To the Indians delight, the Englishmen gave more for pelts than did the French.

Fearing that the Huron and Ottawa might ally themselves with the Iroquois and English, Governor of New France Jacques Brisay Denonville took strong counter measures. He sent Daniel Greysolon Duluth to block

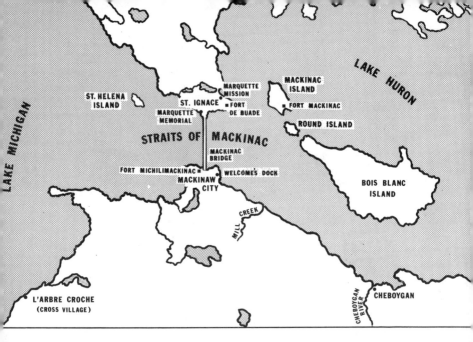

the English route by building Fort St. Joseph on the St. Clair River (near Port Huron, Michigan). Several hundred western warriors led by Olivier Morel de La Durantaye from St. Ignace were dispatched to intercept and capture Roseboom on Lake Huron when he returned in 1687.

England's attack on the French during King William's War (1689-1697) interrupted the flow of furs to Montreal from the west. To protect their post at St. Ignace, the French Commandant Louis de la Porte de Louvigny built Fort de Buade about 1690.

This fort was short-lived. Antoine de la Mothe Sieur de Cadillac assumed command in 1694; Alphonse de Tonty relieved him in 1697. The next year, due to the depressed fur market in France, King Louis XIV ordered the post abandoned and all trade halted. Even though soldiers and officials departed, the *coureurs de bois* continued to trade illegally, and the Jesuits also remained.

To permanently block English expansion into the upper Great Lakes, the King authorized Cadillac to found Fort Pontchartrain at Detroit in 1701. Several thousand western Indians, including the Huron from St. Ignace, were lured to settle along the Detroit River. The Ottawa chose to remain at the Straits.

Michilimackinac Re-established on the South Side of the Straits

French officials soon returned to the Straits. Hoping to stabilize Indian relations and to prevent English intrusions from Hudson's Bay, Governor Philippe de Rigaud Vaudreuil dispatched Constant Le Marchand de Lignery to Michilimackinac in 1712. Lignery, however, had no troops and

30

could not control the forty *coureurs de bois* trading there. He did issue a few trade licenses to demonstrate the government's authority.

Lignery probably began building the new fort after twenty French troops reached Michilimackinac in 1715. He erected the post on the south side of the Straits near the Ottawa, who had recently moved their village to cultivate new fields. Following close behind, the Jesuits re-established the mission of St. Ignace de Michilimackinac.

Despite a popular myth that the French and Indians were the best of friends, the French fought many battles with various Indian tribes. Michilimackinac frequently served as a staging point for military expeditions. In 1715, Lignery prepared for a campaign against the hostile Fox Indians. Several years before, during the winter of 1711-1712, Ottawa and Huron warriors, with French approval, annihilated the Fox village at Detroit. Seeking vengeance, the survivors and their relatives west of Lake Michigan attacked French traders and their Indian allies. The Fox attacks had to be stopped if the fur trade was to continue.

In May 1716, Louis de la Porte Louvigny left Montreal with over 400 Frenchmen and Indians. At Michilimackinac, he recruited the *coureurs de bois* by granting them royal amnesty, and additional Indian warriors. Having secured provisions, Louvigny proceeded to Wisconsin and laid seige to the Fox fort. In the face of a superior force, the Fox agreed to stop fighting. Louvigny, claiming victory, returned to Quebec, but he had achieved only a lull in the hostilities.

Throughout the 1720's, the Fox continued on the warpath, and all efforts to make peace failed. In 1728, Lignery led 1,200 Indians, including 300 Ottawa and Chippewa from Michilimackinac, and more than 400 Frenchmen into Wisconsin to defeat their hated foe. The Fox shrewdly avoided open battle, frustrating the expedition.

After five more exasperating years of conflict, an angry Governor Charles de la Boische de Beauharnois ordered Nicolas Antoine Coulon de Villiers, commandant at Green Bay, to exterminate every Fox. Villiers and Commandant Jean-Baptiste-René Legardeur de Repentigny assembled at Michilimackinac a force of French, Ottawa, Menominee, and Chippewa warriors and paddled on to Green Bay.

Their numbers now depleted, the Fox took refuge in the fortified Sac village at Green Bay. When he arrived, Villiers demanded that the Sac surrender the Fox. They refused. Villiers' men attacked and were repulsed leaving both Villiers and Repentigny dead on the battlefield. Finally, in 1737, Beauharnois gave up his futile attempt to wipe out the remnant of the Fox nation.

Michilimackinac also served as a base for a French expedition south of the Ohio River against the Chickasaw who had been pillaging French boats on the Mississippi. To destroy the Chickasaw, Pierre-Joseph Céloron de Blainville, commandant at Michilimackinac, and some Ottawa accompanied a Canadian contingent that rendezvoused with troops from

Louisiana at Fort L'Assomption (near Memphis, Tennessee) in 1739. Despite some success, the French forces never decisively defeated their enemy.

Not all expeditions leaving Michilimackinac were military. Pierre Gautier de Varennes de la Vérendrye and his sons outfitted at Michilimackinac some of their exploring excursions into the northwest between the 1720's and 1740's.

Michilimackinac was the major depot for the northwestern fur trade. Large canoes, weighted down with brandy, trade goods, and munitions, arrived from Montreal. Traders and voyageurs carried this merchandise on to Indian customers in Michigan, Wisconsin, Minnesota, Ontario, and beyond. Many traders, known as *hivernants*, spent the winter among Indian hunting camps. In spring, they brought their furs to Michilimackinac for shipment to Montreal. At the Straits, they rendezvoused with their friends and recent arrivals from Montreal and spent their wages in a few days of wild celebration.

Since most traders wintered among the Indians, few Frenchmen lived at Michilimackinac all year. In 1749, only ten families and a garrison of about twenty soldiers resided at the fort. Few bothered to raise vegetables. Instead, they subsisted on corn, deer or moose grease, and fish purchased from Indians. Winters, when ice made canoe travel impractical, were long, cold, and lonely.

The Ottawa exhausted their corn fields near the fort after thirty years of cultivation and, in 1741, decided to relocate. To keep them nearby, the French promised to help them clear fields at L'Arbre Croche, twenty five miles to the southwest on Lake Michigan's shore. Since traders at Michilimackinac purchased canoes and large quantities of corn and fat from the Ottawa, the French did not want them to live too far away.

Father Pierre Du Jaunay transferred the Mission of St. Ignace to L'Arbre Croche and ministered there to the 180 warriors and their families. He continued to say mass and to administer sacraments to voyageurs and inhabitants in Ste. Anne's Church. To meet the growing community's spiritual needs, Joseph Ainsse constructed a new edifice in 1743. Du Jaunay financed his mission in part by employing Jean-Baptiste Amiot, a blacksmith, who repaired muskets and iron implements brought in by visiting Indians.

The continuing struggle between the French and English erupted in 1744 into King George's War. In those troubled times, only a few merchants were willing to buy trade licenses. Few trade goods reached Michilimackinac, causing alarm and financial hardship. Fearful of Indian trouble, French soldiers erected a new palisade around the fort.

Their fears were not without foundation. Three years later, Chippewa warriors stabbed two Frenchmen on Mackinac Island, and Ottawa and

FUR TRADE ROUTES TO MICHILIMACKINAC

Chippewa killed cattle and plotted to capture the garrison. The French discovered these plans and barred all Indians from the fort. When Jacques Legardeur de Saint-Pierre assumed command later in the year, he managed to restore order.

War ended in 1748, but aggressive English traders from Pennsylvania pushed into the Ohio country to trade with French allies. George Croghan established a post at Pickawillany (Piqua, Ohio), a Miami town in the heart of Ohio. To end English trade with these Indians, Charles Langlade, nephew of Ottawa Chief LaFourche, led a party of Ottawa and French 400 miles from Michilimackinac in a brilliant raid against Pickawillany in

1752. The dauntless Langlade was a central figure at Michilimackinac during the next half century.

Michilimackinac frequently was the site of large Indian councils. Twelve hundred chiefs and warriors from sixteen tribes, including Huron, Ottawa, Chippewa, Fox, Sac, Miami, Winnebago, Menominee, and Sioux, gathered in 1753 on the ground outside the fort walls. Commandant Louis Liénard de Beaujeu, speaking through interpreters, promised friendship and encouraged the Indians to fight the English. He exchanged strings of wampum and presents with the chiefs. Each nation vowed to follow its French father, but the careful Beaujeu ordered his men to carry their weapons and to have the cannon loaded with grape shot.

The western tribes were essential to the French in their final struggle with Great Britain. Warriors from Michilimackinac helped defeat General Edward Braddock at Fort Duquesne in Pennsylvania in 1755, and the

Birchbark Montreal canoes were the workhorses of the fur trade. Between thirty-five and forty feet long, they carried over three tons of freight plus a crew of at least eight men.

following year Charles Langlade led them east to fight along the frontier from New York to Virginia.

In summer 1757, French and Indian forces captured Fort William Henry, located on the southern tip of Lake Champlain, New York. The joy of victory soon turned to despair. Smallpox from infected English captives was carried back to Michilimackinac and nearby Indian villages. The register of St. Anne's Church contains the names of many men, women, and children, Indian and French, who died from the epidemic.

General James Wolfe struck the fatal blow to New France on the Plains of Abraham at Quebec in September, 1759. The fall of Montreal a year later doomed King Louis XV's North American empire. Langlade and his Indian warriors from Michilimackinac acquitted themselves well at both battles. Canada surrendered and subsequently the Treaty of Paris, 1763 gave all of Canada to Great Britain.

At Michilimackinac, Commandant Beaujeu evacuated the garrison in October 1760 and headed towards Louisiana where the French flag still flew. Charles Langlade was left in command. In less than a year, he had the dubious honor of surrendering Michilimackinac to his lifelong adversary — the English.

The British Take Control

Shortly after the conquest of Canada, General Jeffery Amherst ordered Robert Rogers to take possession of Detroit and Michilimackinac. Rogers reached Detroit in late November, but ice on Lake Huron blocked his passage northward to Michilimackinac. The *fleur-de-lis* would fly another year.

The people of Michilimackinac did not welcome the newly arriving Englishmen. In September 1761, disguised as a French Canadian, Alexander Henry was the first English trader to venture to the Straits. James Stanley Goddard and Ezekiel Solomon soon joined him. Hostile Ottawa threatened to kill them unless they offered favorable trading terms. Fortunately for Henry and his companions, Captain Henry Balfour and a contingent of British troops soon arrived. When Balfour reached Michilimackinac, Charles Langlade turned over the command to him. Balfour informed the villagers that the peace terms permitted the French to retain their property and to practice their Roman Catholic faith. A few days later, Balfour departed, leaving Lieutenant William Leslie of the Sixtieth Regiment, or Royal Americans, in charge of twenty-eight soldiers.

The northern tribes soon became disenchanted with the English. Not understanding the importance to the Indians of exchanging gifts, Amherst, to save money, reduced the quantity of presents and powder given by British officers. At councils, chiefs and warriors sensed an aloofness in the British. Also, English traders seemed intent upon cheating their Indian customers.

Even more ominous to the natives were the white settlers pushing west over the Appalachian Mountains. If they cut down the forest to make farms, the hunting rounds would soon disappear. Some Frenchmen encouraged their former allies to throw off the English yoke.

In spring of 1763, the unrest exploded into a major frontier war known as Pontiac's rebellion. Pontiac was the Ottawa Chief who attacked Detroit and urged his brethren to wipe out the hated English. Indian war parties swiftly captured Fort St. Joseph (Niles, Michigan), Sandusky (Ohio), Fort Miami (Fort Wayne, Indiana), and Fort Ouiatenon (Lafayette, Indiana). Pontiac laid seige to Detroit, but the British, reinforced by troops led by Robert Rogers, held out.

At Michilimackinac, Laurent Ducharme, a Canadian trader, warned Captain George Etherington that local tribesmen planned trouble. Haughtily, Etherington disregarded his advice.

The fort's cannon boomed a salute to commemorate King George III's birthday on 2 June 1763. As part of the celebration, the Chippewa engaged visiting Sac from Wisconsin in a game of *baggitiway*. Etherington and many of his thirty-five soldiers watched the lively contest outside the land gate, but the Chippewa Chief Matchekewis had a surprise for them.

Suddenly a player threw the ball over the fort wall. Warriors raced through the land gate, grabbed weapons from beneath their squaws' blankets and attacked the British troops. Within minutes, they killed sixteen soldiers and captured the rest. Alexander Henry tried to hide in Charles Langlade's garret, but he and the other English traders were apprehended, except for Mr. Tracy who was murdered. Five captured soldiers were later killed, but the remaining captives survived. The French villagers, watching in horror, were unable to help since the Indians quarrel was not with them.

For over a year, the Canadians managed the fort without the arrogant British. But on 22 September 1764, Captain William Howard re-garrisoned the fort with two companies of the Seventeenth Regiment. The English had come to stay.

Possessed by a burning desire to discover a northwest water passage to the Pacific Ocean, Robert Rogers arrived at Michilimackinac on 10 August 1766. While in London a year earlier, he had secured a royal commission as commandant. Rogers, his wife Elizabeth Browne, and two companies of the Sixtieth Regiment came on board the Schooner *Gladwin* to Michilimackinac in 1764 — the first sailing vessel to call at the Straits since the ill-fated *Griffin*.

Rogers dispatched James Tute and Jonathan Carver, French and Indian War veterans from Massachusetts, to search for a passage to the Orient. Carver departed for the Mississippi on 3 September; and two weeks later, Tute and James Stanley Goddard followed. They rendezvoused at the Falls of St. Anthony (Minneapolis, Minnesota) where Tute assumed command with Carver serving as cartographer. Failing to explore any new territory or to find the elusive passage, they returned a year later to a disappointed Rogers at Michilimackinac.

Troubled by the debt from Tute's mission, Rogers was beset with a more serious problem. On 6 December 1767, Captain Frederick Spies-macher and a file of soldiers arrested him. Accused of treasonable plotting with French and Spanish officials, the famous hero spent the winter in the guardhouse. In spring Rogers again rode the *Gladwin*, this time his legs in irons, enroute to Montreal for trial. Though he was acquitted, his reputation was ruined.

FORT MICHILIMACKINAC

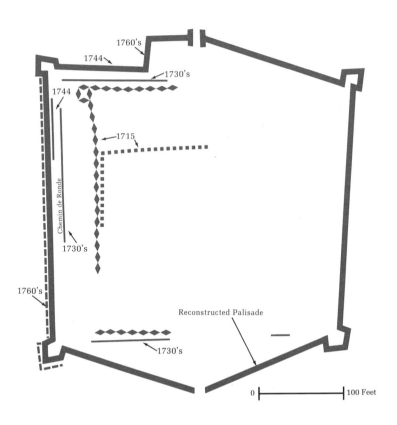

Expansions of the Fort's stockade as revealed by archaeology.

Even though Great Britain controlled Michilimackinac, French traders continued to trade in the northwestern wilderness. From the Spanish
port of New Orleans they imported goods and exported furs by way of the
Mississippi. British regulations prohibited traders from wintering among
Indians and required Indians to bring their pelts to Michilimackinac. This
caused losses for English traders and great inconvenience for Indians.
Finally, in 1769, the traders were allowed to winter in Indian country.

For years, rich copper deposits near the southern shore of Lake
Superior enticed explorers. French attempts in the 1730's to exploit this
wealth proved futile. Hoping for more success in the early 1770's, English
businessman Alexander Baxter teamed with Alexander Henry, Henry
Bostwick, and Jean Baptiste Cadot in a mining enterprise. They also failed
by 1774.

For the fur trade to prosper, it was essential that Indian tribes be at
peace with each other. When disputes arose, the post commandant tried to
settle them before they resulted in bloodshed. In 1774, hostilities broke out
between the Chippewa and their ancient foe, the Sioux. Captain Arent
Schuyler De Peyster, the new commandant, ordered Peter Pond and other
traders who wintered among these tribes to bring chiefs and warriors from
both nations to Michilimackinac for a council.

When they arrived, De Peyster held a "Grand Council." He handed out
presents to his visitors and extracted promises from both sides to live
peacefully with each other and to protect the traders among them. The
commandants at Michilimackinac found conducting Indian diplomacy to
be their most difficult and frustrating task.

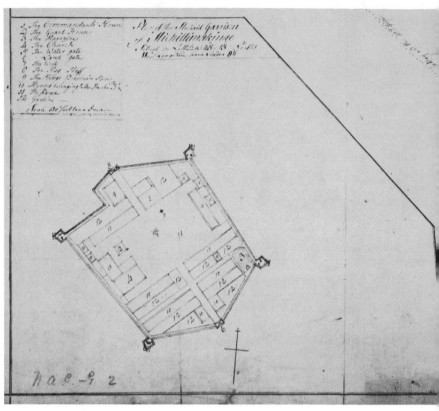

1760's map of Michilimackinac
Courtesy - Public Record Office, London

Skirmishes between British troops and angry colonists at Lexington and Concord in Massachusetts in the spring of 1775 portended trouble for Michilimackinac. As the rebellion spread, it threatened Michilimackinac's existence. American rebels captured Montreal in November 1776, and it seemed likely that no trade goods would be sent west. British troops drove the invaders out of Canada and sufficient merchandise reached Michilimackinac to avert economic disaster.

The American Revolution profoundly affected life at Michilimackinac. Each year, John Askin and his fellow traders struggled to import sufficient goods to meet Indian demands. Except for declines in 1776 and 1779, trade flourished throughout the war. In 1778, 128 canoes brought over 2,100 kegs of rum and brandy, 1,500 muskets, 28 tons of gunpowder, 35 tons of shot and ball, and hundreds of bales of trade goods to be exchanged for furs. In addition, the *Welcome, Felicity,* and *Archange* carried provisions from Detroit. Thousands of pelts were sent back to Montreal for export to Europe.

Keeping the trade routes open was essential to British interests at Michilimackinac, for an active trade kept Indians loyal to the British. George Rogers Clark, a Virginian, led a rebel force into Illinois and Indiana and aided by pro-American French inhabitants, captured the posts of Vincennes, Kaskaskia, and Cahokia and threatened Michilimackinac. He swiftly gained the active support of neutrality or neighboring tribes. West of the Mississippi at St. Louis, the Spanish, too, encouraged Indians to oppose Britain.

The British boasted that only they could supply Indian needs for blankets, kettles, muskets, lead, and gunpowder. Yet they saw some old friends — Potawatomi, Sac, and Fox turn against them. Even the nearby Ottawa and Chippewa wavered in their devotion to King George III.

Both DePeyster and his successor, Lieutenant Governor Patrick Sinclair exhausted themselves trying to keep the Indians loyal. Their agents, Charles Langlade and Charles Gautier recruited war parties from the Sioux, Menominee, Winnebago, Sac, Fox, Ottawa, and Chippewa nations. These warriors traveled great distances to fight the American rebels:

1776 — to Montreal to help defend Canada
1777 — to aid General John Burgoyne at Saratoga, New York
1778 — to fight in Canada again
1779   to St. Joseph (Niles, Michigan) to resist an anticipated rebel advance against Detroit from Illinois
1780 — to attack unsuccessfully the Spanish post at St. Louis
1782 — to help defeat Daniel Boone at Blue Licks, Kentucky

War parties numbered in the hundreds, and the King paid dearly for their services. The Crown outfitted the warriors, provided provisions for their families, and re-supplied the men when they returned. In addition, they provided expensive presents to the chiefs.

Indian moccasin from Michilimackinac acquired by Arent Schuyler De Peyster. Courtesy City of Liverpool Museums.

Despite the tremendous expense of the Indian allies, the military accomplishments were small. By the time the Indians arrived in Canada in 1776 and 1778, they were no longer needed; and when they took the battlefield, British officers found them undisciplined. British authorities in Canada, strapped for funds, complained bitterly about expenditures for Indians at Michilimackinac. Finally, they forced Patrick Sinclair to relinquish his command in 1782.

When Sinclair relieved De Peyster in October 1779, he had already decided to move the community to Mackinac Island. If George Rogers Clark launched a naval assault from Lake Michigan, the wooden stockade could not withstand cannon fire. Even more threatening, the Ottawa and Chippewa were showing contempt for the English, and the memory of 1763 still lingered. Although the French inhabitants remained loyal to the British Crown, British officers worried they might embrace the rebel cause when France, in 1778, became an official ally of the fledgling United States.

Mackinac Island possessed a fine natural harbor. On the mainland, ships had to drop anchor several hundred yards away from shore to unload passengers and cargo into batteaux. In winter 1779-80, the residents of Michilimackinac dismantled their church, transported the logs over the ice, and re-erected it on the island. On the island, the civilian community was separated from the fort. Ste. Anne's Church and all private houses were located along the shoreline beneath the bluff where the fort stood 150 feet above the water. For the next few years, the move continued. The *Welcome* ferried over inhabitants and their possessions. Sinclair employed voyageurs to assist his soldiers in constructing Fort Mackinac. Among the fort's buildings were the barracks, guardhouse, and provisions storehouse which were brought over from Michilimackinac.

In July 1781, one-half the garrison moved into Fort Mackinac. The remainder followed a short time later. Two years later, all the effort expended in this transfer appeared to be in vain for the peace treaty ending the Revolution gave Mackinac Island to the new United States. British troops, however, occupied it until 1796 when American soldiers took possession as a result of Jay's treaty. During the War of 1812, British forces recaptured the Island but returned it at war's end. Since 1815, Mackinac Island has been undisputed American territory.

Michilimackinac was abandoned. Only a few crumbling buildings and rotting palisades remained. Windblown sand gradually covered the remnants of the once thriving community. In 1857 when the present day village of Mackinaw City was platted, the site of the fort was designated a public park. The village turned over the land to the state in 1904 to become Michigan's second state park. Park workmen discovered remains of the palisades, and the stockade was reconstructed during the 1930's.

Today the fort is being resurrected by the Mackinac Island State Park Commission to help visitors recapture the excitement of a bygone era.

Archaeology at Michilimackinac

Every summer since 1959 skilled archaeologists have painstakingly revealed Michilimackinac's buried past. Digging with small trowels, they carefully cut back the layers of the soil. Stains in the soil left by building foundations and fence lines are recorded. As one year's information is added to the next, the location of houses and their property lines are plotted.

To date a little more than half of the fort has been excavated, and a few buildings in the extensive suburbs outside the fort walls have been located.

All dirt is patiently sifted so that even the smallest artifact can be retrieved. Thus far more than a million eighteenth century items have been found. Each button, bead, china dish, and gun part tells its own rich story of life on the frontier at Michilimackinac.

The walls of the fort and the reconstructed buildings stand on the exact site of the originals as revealed by archaeologists. Many of the excavated artifacts are on display within the fort. Some large features such as

Turlington's
"Balsam of Life"
bottle

Pewter enlisted man's button

a French well, a storage cellar, the powder magazine floor and a stone chimney have been left as they were found.

Each summer from mid-June to Labor Day visitors may watch the Mackinac State Historic Parks', archaeologists at work.

During the winter the archaeologists write reports of their excavations. A list of many illustrated archaeological publications is available at the Visitor Center or by mail.

Diorama of LaSalle's Griffin which sailed to Michilimackinac in 1679

Old Mackinac Point Lighthouse

Built in 1892, the Old Mackinac Point Light helped guide ships through the straits until 1957. Both the keeper and his assistant and their families lived here. Throughout its sixty-six years of operation only four keepers served: George W. Marshall, 1892-1919; James M. Marshall, 1919-1940; Henrik Olsen, 1940-1946; and John Campbell, 1946-1957.

For Further Reading

Extensive historical and archaeological research is being conducted in conjunction with the reconstruction of Fort Michilimackinac. The Mackinac State Historic Parks has published the findings of much of this work:

Attack at Michilimackinac, 1763: Alexander Henry's Travels and Adventures in Canada and the Indian Territories between the years 1760 and 1764 (1971), 131 pp., ed. by David A. Armour.

At the Crossroads; Michilimackinac During the American Revolution (1978), 279 pp. by David A. Armour and Keith R. Widder.

David and Elizabeth: The Mitchell Family of the Straits of Mackinac (1982), 12 pp. by David A. Armour.

The Doctor's Secret Journal (1960), 47 pp., ed. by George S. May.

Firearms on the Frontier: Guns at Fort Michilimackinac (1976), 39 pp. by T. M. Hamilton.

Fort Michilimackinac in 1749 (1976), 12 pp. trans. and ed. by Marie Gerin-Lajoie.

Fort Michilimackinac Sketch Book (1988), 64 pp. by David A. Armour with drawings by Dirk Gringhuis, Patricia Hogg and Eric Manders.

Fort Michilimackinac 1715-1781: An Archaeological Perspective on the Revolutionary Frontier, pub. with the Museum, Michigan State University (1974), 367 pp., by Lyle M. Stone.

France at Mackinac: A Pictorial Record of French Life and Culture 1715-1760 (1968), 38 pp., by Eugene T. Petersen.

Gentlemen on the Frontier: A Pictorial Record of the Culture of Michilimackinac (1964), 66 pp., by Eugene T. Petersen (out of print).

Indian Costume at Mackinac: Seventeenth and Eighteenth Century (1972), 12 pp., by Dirk Gringhuis.

Lore of the Great Turtle: Indian Legends of Mackinac Retold (1970), 89 pp., by Dirk Gringhuis.

Mackinac and the Porcelain City (1985), 40 pp., by Eugene T. Petersen.

Mackinac History, Vol. I: An Informal Series of Illustrated Vignettes (1969), 12 illustrated vignettes (out of print).

Milestones of the Past: Military Buttons and Insignia from Mackinac (1975), 12 pp., by Brian Leigh Dunnigan.

The Powder Magazine at Fort Michilimackinac: Excavation Report (1977) 32 pp., by Donald P. Heldman and William L. Minnerly.

Treason? at Michilimackinac: The Proceedings of a General Court Martial held at Montreal in October 1768 for the Trial of Major Robert Rogers (1972), 107 pp., ed. by David A. Armour.

Were-Wolves and Will-O-The-Wisps: French Tales of Mackinac Retold (1974), 106 pp., by Dirk Gringhuis.

The Young Voyageur (1969), 202 pp., by Dirk Gringhuis.

Archaeological Completion Report Series

Archaeological Investigations at French Farm Lake in Northern Michigan, 1981-1982: A British Colonial Farm Site (1983), 142 pp., by Donald P. Heldman.

Colonial Nails from Michilimackinac: Differentiation by Chemical and Statistical Analysis (1983), 83 pp., by David J. Frurip, Russell Malewicki, and Donald P. Heldman.

Eighteenth-Century Gunflints from Fort Michilimackinac and Other Colonial Sites (1988), 281 pp., by T. M. Hamilton and K. O. Emery.

Excavations at Fort Michilimackinac, 1976: The Southeast and South Southeast Row Houses (1977), 264 pp. by Donald P. Heldman (out of print).

Excavations at Fort Michilimackinac, 1977: House One of the South Southeast Row Houses (1978), 234 pp. by Donald P. Heldman (out of print).

Excavations at Fort Michilimackinac, 1978-1979: The Rue de la Babillarde (1981), 470 pp., by Donald P. Heldman and Roger T. Grange, Jr.

Excavations at Fort Michilimackinac, 1983-1985: House C of the Southeast Row House, The Solomon-Levy-Parant House (1985), 215 pp., by Jill Y. Halchin.

French Subsistence at Fort Michilimackinac, 1715-1781: The Clergy and the Traders (1985), 218 pp., by Elizabeth M. Scott.

Jesuit Rings from Fort Michilimackinac and Other European Contact Sites (1983), 66 pp., by Judith Ann Hauser.

Lead Seals from Fort Michilimackinac, 1715-1761 (1989), 48 pp., by Diane L. Adams.

The Mill Creek Site and Pattern Recognition in Historial Archaelogy (1985), 265 pp., by Patrick E. Martin.

A Search for the Eighteenth Century Village at Michilimackinac: A Soil Resistivity Survey (1982), 79 pp., by J. Mark Williams and Gary Shapiro.

All of these publications are available from the Mackinac State Historic Parks, Box 873, Mackinaw City, Michigan 49701.

A Visit to Mackinac Island

Visitors today, like those of the nineteenth century, can visit beautiful Mackinac Island. Over eighty per cent of this car-free and picturesque island is Mackinac Island State Park. Arch Rock, Sugar Loaf, Fort Holmes, and a host of other natural wonders inspire thousands each year. A stroll along the wooded paths, a bicycle ride around the island, or just a deep breath of fresh Mackinac air can help revitalize the human spirit. A number of self-directed tour routes begin at the State Park visitor center.

Fortunately much of the island's past has been preserved. Since Patrick Sinclair's workmen first built Fort Mackinac, the limestone fortification has stood guard over the straits. Throughout over a century of military occupation, the fort underwent numerous renovations. In 1958, the Mackinac State Historic Parks began systematically to restore it, and today Fort Mackinac appears as it did in the 1880's. Interpretive displays in buildings and costumed interpreters bring back much of the fort's rich heritage.

The Mackinac State Historic Parks also maintains and operates the Indian Dormitory, Benjamin Blacksmith Shop, Beaumont Memorial, Biddle House, McGulpin House and the Mission Church.